The UGLY T Hitting Ground-Balls: How To Choose Baseball Hitting Drills For Kids

THE UGLY TRUTH ABOUT HITTING GROUND-BALLS: HOW TO CHOOSE BASEBALL HITTING DRILLS FOR KIDS

How To Choose Baseball Hitting Drills For Kids

Joey Myers

CONTENTS

PLEASE REVIEW ON AMAZON

Thank you for downloading my book, please review on Amazon so we can make future versions even better.

ACKNOWLEDGEMENTS

First and foremost I have to **thank my most loving and supportive wife and family**. I spent many of nights on a deadline, to get this book done, alone in our bedroom hacking away at the keyboard.

Tiffany Myers, who **I'm lucky to have snagged before some other hairy-backed-knuckle-dragger**, and with over 9 years of marriage, you complete me.

This is also for my 4 year old son Noah, and 10 month old daughter Gracen. You guys will learn the value of hard work on whatever passionate curiosity you find yourself in. Mommy and Daddy will help keep providing oxygen to that fire making it as big as you want it.

I want to thank Rann Dasco for the beautiful front and back cover design. You did a fantastic job girlie! ?

I also wanted to thank the coaches who helped me make this viral "thing" what it is. Your advice both positive or constructive was equally appreciated.

INTRODUCTION

PLEASE NOTE that even though I labeled this a "baseball hitting drills for kids" book, it's not going to give you drills. The objective of this book is to guide coaches in **picking "effective" drills to help kids get the ball in the air**. In other words, I'm teaching you HOW TO fish.

CAUTION: this is a RANT to end all rants, REVEAL-ING the ugly truth about teaching hitters to consistently hit ground-balls. You're in for a wild ride, so please proceed with caution...

—

Right off the bat (pun intended),

I'm going to pick a fight, and upset some people in talking about The UGLY Truth About Hitting Ground-balls: Baseball Hitting Drills For Kids...

So here goes.

Drum roll please...

Teaching Baseball Hitting Drills For Kids To Primarily Hit Ground Balls Is Idiotic & DOES NOT Make Sense

What do you think of that? Fired up?! If so, then GOOD.

Okay, so this *UGLY Truth About Hitting Ground-balls RANT* has been brewing in me for some time now...

AND it came to a boil when I promoted the BackSpin batting tee swing experiment blog post on Facebook, titled *"Baseball Batting Cage Drills: A Quick Way To Hit Less Ground-balls"* (http://gohpl.com/backspinteex)...

You can click the following link to read all the "classic" Facebook comments posted to the BackSpin Tee promo:

http://bit.ly/backspincomments

A flood of baseball hitting drills for kids Facebook comments came in, mostly from coaches...High School to College...baseball to softball...chiming in about **how effective it is to teach their hitters** to hit the ball on the ground, and claiming how terrible of an idea the Backspin Tee is promoting more line drives and productive batted balls in the air.

And by the way, a line drive is a ball in the air!

They go on and on about:

- How many games they've won with grounders,
- How fielding percentage is way lower than fly-balls,
- That it's much easier to catch a fly ball,
- How great outfielders track fly balls,
- How **more can go wrong with the defense** keeping the ball on the ground,
- If their team hit more grounders, then they'd score more runs,
- How some of the most winningest coaches in college baseball history, Gordie Gillespie and Augie Garrido as examples, stress keeping the ball on the ground to their hitters,
- How you HAVE TO TEACH a 5'6", 135-pound High School hitter to hit the ball on the ground because his batted ball distance maxes out at 250-feet! And,

- How even pro coaches and "great hitting instructors" never promote hitting fly-balls.

And for your information, these comments will be our Chapters going forward.

For those fired up by my statement above...

Does that about cover ALL your arguments for WHY hitting a ground-ball is far superior than putting a ball in the air?

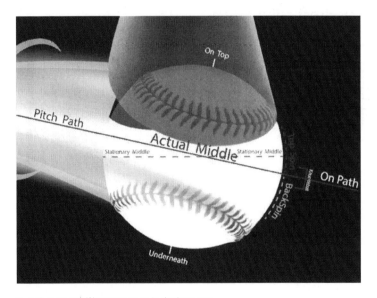

On Path, Bottom Half image courtesy: Backspintee.com

By the way, **those arguments WILL look like swiss cheese** in a moment.

But before I get there, and even more disturbing...

You Don't Put Backspin on a Ball by Swinging Down

Some, but not all, of the past Facebook comments shared how to put consistent backspin on the ball by swinging down on it...

The keyword here is "consistent".

They even go so far as to believe that young hitters HAVE TO swing down on the ball to get backspin because they're not "strong enough" to put backspin on it like Major League hitters!!

Wa!!?

I want you to go to YouTube and search for a video with the following keywords, "MLB Homerun Derby 2014 Highlights (all the homeruns)", and please **note which part of the ball these guys are hitting** (top half or bottom half?)...on-path bottom half is the answer.

NEWS FLASH! This is just as true for young small hitters, as it is for MLB hitters. It's **written into the rules** of Physics. Can't break those rules if you're on earth, sorry.

And if YOU STILL don't believe me, read this MLB article titled, *"Jon Lester Shows Importance Of Launch Angle":* http://gohpl.com/jonlesterlaunchangle. The article goes onto to say how Lester ranks second among Major League hitting pitchers with an average Ball Exit Speed of 92.5-mph.

So, what's the problem?

Quoted from the article:

> *"...(He ended up with four hits on the season in 71 plate appearances, a .065/.108/.065 line.) Part of it is that, like many pitchers, contact was an issue — **Lester's 42.3 percent strikeout rate** was above the 37.7 percent average for pitchers."*

How could Lester hit the ball so hard without finding much hitting success?

Again, quoted from the article:

> *"...it's because 19 of Lester's 24 tracked batted balls failed to get above 7 degrees of launch angle. Sixteen of those 19*

failed to even achieve positive launch angle, which is to say
*that **he pounded the ball into the ground constantly.**"*

We "in the biz" call these 'worm-burners'.

In other words, to get the ball in the air, the hitter MUST have a positive launch angle. Translated? The barrel MUST be traveling UP to impact for consistent backspin to occur *(revisit Backspin Tee 'On Path Bottom Half' graphic above)*. NOT down!

If the hitter has a negative launch angle (barrel traveling down to impact), THEY WILL:

1. Put topspin on the ball which will cause the ball to dive and NOT carry,

2. Strikeout more,

3. NOT get many hits, and

4. Professionally speaking, **NOT make it past A-ball** *(if they're lucky enough to make it that far)*.

One last thing about baseball hitting drills for kids point #4 above, Aaron Miles (http://www.baseball-reference.com/players/m/milesaa01.shtml), who played 12 years of professional baseball (9 years in the Big Leagues with White Sox, Cardinals, Rockies, and Dodgers), told me these downward swing path hitters got weeded out by AA-ball.

By the way, Aaron Miles is 5'7", 180-lbs, which is impressive that with his size he competed for 9 Major Leagues seasons and did quite well. You don't play that long in the Big Leagues, with his size, UNLESS you're doing something right. Success leaves clues right?!

Am I making myself clear on this 'down swinging' backspin issue? Side note, aside, before I go into crushing the "Pro-Ground-baller" arguments, I want to **get something out of the way first**...

Hitting Ground-balls have their Place

...in situational hitting, which depending on how the game goes, can make up between 5 to 10% of a team's at-bats. Of course, we don't want to put a ball in the air on a hit-and-run or with slap hit. That's moronic. Even I know that, and I've been told on social media that I have a slightly below average human intelligence. ? lol

What I have a beef with are coaches **teaching hitters to hit the ball on the ground**...ALL THE TIME! Using this as their primary hitting objective. And, by the way, HERE'S THE KICKER...

DID YOU KNOW...

Line drives are balls in the air? Doesn't take a physics professor to see that.

What's more...

Pitchers Want Hitters Hitting the Ball on the Ground!

What vertical part of the zone do pitching coaches teach their pitchers to primarily use?

"Keep the ball down!"...is what they'll say.

Now, **what part of the ball are pitchers HOPING hitters hit by keeping the ball down?**

That's right! The <u>TOP HALF OF THE BALL</u>.

Because, as the Backspin Tee 'On Path Bottom Half' graphic above shows, hitting the top half of the ball induces a top spin, creating more worm burners. In other words, PITCHERS WANT HITTERS TO HIT THE BALL ON THE GROUND!!!

It's all about seeking pleasure and avoiding pain. Pitchers know that they don't get hurt (as much) with a ground-ball than with a ball-in-the-air. So **WHY the heck are hitting coaches teaching their hitters to primarily hit ground-balls?!**

You following me here?

Or is this some LARGE conspiracy of pitching instructors undermining our hitters? Let me give you another bit of baseball hitting drills for kids advice: Don't listen to pitching coaches teach hitting. Unless, they're aware of this strange duality between pitching and hitting strategy. You see, they've been conditioned to induce ground-balls, so whether they're conscious about it or not, to hitters, **they're promoting the VERY THING they use to get hitters out.** Most of the pitching instructors in my area, who also teach hitting, instruct their hitters to swing down on the ball.

Coincidence?

Click the following link for a Beyond the Boxscore article titled, *"Scooter Gennett and ground balls"*. The subtitle says it all, *"Scooter Gennett's offense has declined every year since he broke into Major League Baseball, are ground balls the reason?"*: http://gohpl.com/sgennettgbs

Okay, moving on...

Before getting into picking apart each of the individual "Pro-Ground-ballers" arguments, I included at the beginning of this post, I want you to answer the following question...

Which is Better? A Ground Ball Pitcher or a Fly Ball Pitcher

Let's wet the whistle with a FanGraphs.com article titled, *"Which is Better? A Ground Ball Pitcher or a Fly Ball Pitcher"*: http://gohpl.com/gborflyball...this article is an interesting MUST READ for all. However, one graphic I wanted to **draw your attention to,** is this one:

they're just different.

Let's take a look at a little bit of data to get started. Here are the results on each type of ball in play from 2014:

Type	AVG	ISO	wOBA
GB	.239	.020	.220
LD	.685	.190	.684
FB	.207	.378	.335

AVG = Batting Average, ISO = "Isolated Slugging%" or Raw Power, & wOBA = weighted On-Base AVG. Baseball hitting drills for kids graph compliments of FanGraphs.com

What's obvious in the results, for each type of ball in play, is the value of the Line Drive (highlighted in yellow). I think even "Pro-Ground-baller" coaches agree that line drives are the way to go.

But if given a choice to pick the lesser of two evils, the Pro-Ground-ball coach will unanimously pick the ground-ball.

But look at the difference in productivity between the Ground-ball and Fly-ball...

- A 32-point increase in Batting Average with Ground-ball over a Fly-ball, however
- A **358-point INCREASE** in ISO (or raw power) with Fly-balls over Ground-balls...AND
- A **115-point INCREASE** in weighted On-Base Average* with Fly-Balls over Ground-balls, which according to FanGraphs.com,

*"Weighted On-Base Average combines all the different aspects of hitting into one metric, weighting each of them in proportion to their actual run value. While batting average, on-base percentage, and slugging percentage fall short in accuracy and scope, wOBA measures and captures offensive value more accurately and comprehensively."

Well Fly-balls, it's unanimous...2 out of 3 will get you in the Hall Of Fame ? lol Also, since we're on the subject, Click the following Twitter link to check out this Launch Angle info-graphic of Bryce Harper that was posted by @PinkmanBaseball: http://bit.ly/bharperlaunch

Oh HAPPY DAY! Key in on Bryce Harper's offensive productivity from 10 to 30-degrees of Launch Angle! Did you pick up on the KEY message? Killed two birds with one stone there...

- **Key Message #1:** This shows hitters aren't productive unless they're swinging UP to the ball (not down)...
- **Key Message #2:** And if a 9-degree Launch Angle, or less (*see 'Backspin' image #2 above*), is a ground-ball, WATCH how B. Harper's average AND power numbers skyrocket once he gets to over a 10-degree Launch Angle.

Situational hitting aside, remind me again <u>WHY we're teaching</u> baseball hitting drills for kids that promote grounders?

So far, I hope this has helped the 'fence-sitters' see the light...now, let's **zero in on those not even close to the fence**. You know who you are. I may not get you over to the 'Light Side' reading this whole post...BUT, the information will fester in your single-minded brain, like an open wound...and with time, I'm confident you'll make your way to the Lighter Side of effective hitting.

Don't worry, **I'll be a patient grasshopper**. I don't care what level of play you coach. YOU WILL BE MINE Ferris Bueller!

Photo courtesy: FoundItemClothing.com

Onwards...
The "Pro-Ground-ballers", go on and on about...

1

ARGUMENT #1: HOW MANY GAMES WE'VE WON WITH GROUNDERS

This is a subjective statement, and an exaggeration at BEST.

I mean, of all the baseball and softball games being played on the planet, **how many late inning heroic game winners** are being hit on the ground?

AND, of those game winning ground-balls, how many of those WERE INTENDED to be on the ground by the hitter and/or coach?

Here's what I want ALL coaches to do...

Track your game winning hits, and report back.

Don't cheat though "Pro-Ground-ballers", and **fudge the numbers to save face**.

My hypothesis is, ground-balls WILL NOT be the number one game winning vehicle.

I've seen too many game winning balls-in-the-air (line drives and fly-balls), in my playing career, to accept that ground-balls get the job done better.

The "Pro-Ground-ballers", go on and on about…

2

ARGUMENT #2: HOW GROUND-BALL FIELDING PERCENTAGE IS WAY LOWER THAN WITH FLY-BALLS

This statement **proves a statistically flawed argument**. Here's the information that we need to put it to the test:

The New York Mets infield plays a defensive shift against Carlos Gonzalez of the Colorado Rockies at Coors Field on April 16, 2013 in Denver, Colorado. (Baseball hitting drills for kids photo by Doug Pensinger/Getty Images)

- Total number of ground-balls hit in 2015 MLB season, and
- Total number of fly-balls hit 2015 MLB season.

I'm willing to bet, there were WAY more ground-balls hit than fly-balls in 2015.

More statistical data points translate to lower overall averages. And the reverse is typically true of less statistical information.

Riddle me this,

...if fielding percentages for outfielders are higher, then **WHY don't we teach our pitchers to pitch to the top of zone**, than the bottom?

Doesn't that sound logical?..."*Hey, if our outfielders are the better fielders, then get hitters to hit more balls to them.*"

Here's what I thought up ALL BY MYSELF,

There are FIVE fielding infielders (including the pitcher), and only THREE outfielders.

There's more space in the outfield and less fielders…WHY don't we hit it out there?

Even my four year old can see the superiority in that baseball hitting drills for kids strategy.

One of my readers Brian Ingram, shared this:

> "Just read the article about the flawed ground ball approach and wanted to say I completely agree. also wanted to add on to the idea of 5 infielders vs 3 outfielders, (which I thought of too as soon as I read the title and was happy you touched on it) was that those **5 infielders have less total area to cover on ground balls than the 3 outfielders do on balls in the air.**
>
> And the space where ground balls get through is far smaller than the area where balls in the air go for hits. Also, like you showed in the article, ground balls are either hard or soft. Balls in the air though can be shallow line drives, deep line drives, deep fly balls, and bloop hits.
>
> In addition, higher chance of getting on base from things like bad reads, ball getting lost in the sun or lights, wind issues, knuckling line drives, etc.
>
> Also outfielders have a limit of the outfield fence on how far they can go back to catch a ball. Infielders don't have to deal with those issues, which also count as hits not errors leading to the discrepancy in fielding percentage. All of those things taken into consideration **leads to the conclusion that odds of reaching base safely is much high** hitting the ball in the air than on the ground. All in all I loved the article and couldn't agree more."

Thanks for sharing that Brian (*who's applying to be in the Kinesiology Department at Fresno State in the Fall*).

Did I mention this was a RANT?!

Here's another thought to consider (*referring to the superiority of fielding percentages in the outfield*),

In using a defensive shift, **WHY would we put an extra**

infielder into the outfield, if the outfielders – statistically speaking – were better at fielding?

They don't NEED anymore help!

Because according to you, outfielders HAVE TO BE BETTER fielders than infielders right? That's what the stats tell us!!!

Yoda (The Force) photo courtesy: BusinessInsider.com

Or how about this...

Since we shifted the infielder positionally into the outfield, does he/she instantaneously inherit the stellar fielding percentage of playing on the luscious outfield grass?

Sounds like "the Force" in Star Wars ? haha

Statistically speaking, **comparing an infielders fielding percentage to an outfielders is comparing apples to oranges**.

Are we done here? Good.

The "Pro-Ground-ballers", go on and on about...

3

ARGUMENT #3: IT'S MUCH EASIER TO CATCH A FLY BALL

Is it?

Steps to processing a ground-ball:

> 1. Field it,
> 2. Throw it,
> 3. Catch it.

Steps to processing a fly-ball:

1. Move under it,
2. Catch it.

Hey look! One less step! You may be onto something here…

But are you?

I played the outfield from my sophomore year in High School through all 4-years at Fresno State, so I know how easy AND difficult it is.

Again, you're one of three fielders in the biggest part of a baseball or softball field.

Ask Jose Canseco **how easy it is to catch this "fly ball"** after watching this video on YouTube searching with the keywords, *"Martinez homer aided by Canseco's head"*. You've probably already seen it.

Also, ask an infielder going back to catch a fly-ball in the shallow outfield, with a converging outfielder coming towards them, how easy catching that fly-ball is.

At Fresno State, legendary Coach Bob Bennett (https://en.wikipedia.org/wiki/Bob_Bennett_(baseball)) constantly had us working on this type of drill called "Pop-fly Priorities". We were drilled to the point of throwing up, AND even still, occasionally **the ball dropped into 'no-man's land'** in games.

I'd love to take the "Pro-Ground-ballers" out and hit you fly-balls, and have you track them down. They're much harder to track than you think. And things move A LOT faster in the outfield, most of the time you're on a dead sprint to get from point A to B.

And, when an outfielder makes a mistake, runners advance at least one extra base. If infielders bobble a ball, typically, they still have time to recover and get the out. In other words, **an outfielder's mistake is magnified.**

Besides, my friends who've played in the Big Leagues say the outfield is where misfit infielders go, which brings the quality of overall outfield play down at the highest level. Ask any converted outfielder how challenging it is to track a ball effectively off a bat ?

Which leads me to,

The "Pro-Ground-ballers", go on and on about...

4

ARGUMENT #4: HOW GREAT OUTFIELDERS TRACK FLY BALLS

But you're thinking, well, MLB and college outfielders (both baseball and softball) are great athletes, and they track and catch everything in the air.

They don't. Not even 'cans-of-corn' are off limits to being dropped.

Don't believe me? Go to YouTube and type in "mlb dropped fly ball", and count how many, what you think are 'cans-of-corns', are dropped.

And for you college coaches who still don't agree...?

This season, **track how many balls are dropped by your outfielders** this year...AND the result of that action.

Then track how many ground-balls are dropped by your infielders this year...AND the result of that action.

My point is, **NOT ALL fly-balls to outfielders are caught**, and when they aren't, extra bases are taken. Heck, extra bases are taken if an outfielder takes a bit too long fielding a line drive/ground-ball in front of them!

If an infielder drops a ball, most of the time, it's no big deal, at least if the runner isn't fleet of foot. All is forgiven, minimal damage done. Not outfielders, no-no.

The "Pro-Ground-ballers", go on and on about...

5

ARGUMENT #5: MORE CAN GO WRONG WITH THE DEFENSE KEEPING THE BALL ON THE GROUND

My good friend Taylor Gardner, and owner of the Back-Spin batting tee, shared a CLASSIC baseball hitting drills for kids response to the aforementioned statement on Facebook (*and one I echoed earlier in this post*). He said:

*"Groundball supporters...why do pitchers try and keep the ball down in the zone? ....They WANT you to hit a groundball. If you don't believe that, then start telling your pitchers to live about chest high in the zone and see how many pop ups you can get in the game. Ha ha...you should bring your center fielder into the infield and play with an extra infielder because **you seem to be so scared of the groundballs** (which are better right)?"*

This is a common argument amongst Little League coaches...

"Hit the ball on the ground because the other team can't play catch!"

But **what happens when they meet a team that can play catch?** What then?

Spoiler ALERT! They get beat. And IF they get a runner on base, then they're another ground-ball away from a double play!!!

If the other team can play catch, no more getting runners on base because of errors...no more auto-runs to second after a walk. NOTHING. Your team is DONE.

This is WHY, when and if my 4yo son plays baseball, his team will be the most disciplined group of young men at playing catch. If I come across YOUR ground-ball hitting team, we will CRUSH YOU. **You better have quality pitching,** because YOU WILL LOSE!

And you won't know how it happened...why it happened...or what happened. Well, if you've read this, then you will know what happened, and shame on you for not seeing the writing on the wall beforehand...trick me once, shame on you, but trick me twice, shame on me!! lol

Worst of all, your troops won't be able to recover

because you've taught them baseball hitting drills for kids that primarily focus on hitting the ball on the ground.

Have you ever been in a hopeless situation like that? It's only a matter of time, if you keep doing what you're doing.

What's more,

Guess **what happens to ground-ball fielding difficulty** after graduating to the BIG field...?

> 1. Infielders are deeper – increasing their fielding range,
> 2. Athletes get more athletic – enabling them a farther "reach",
> 3. Players get better at playing catch (skill acquisition), and
> 4. With 90-foot bases (instead of 60 to 70-foot), fielders have more time to field, gather, and throw. In other words, more can go wrong with fielding a ground-ball, and the defense still recording a putout because they have more time.

But you "Pro-Ground-Baller" Little League coaches don't care anyway, **it'll be the next coaches problem** when they get into Middle School.

Fastpitch softball is a little different...the young ladies will grow into the "smaller" field. However, points ONE through THREE above still hold true.

One last baseball hitting drills for kids point I want to make on this, comes from a *Beyond The Box Score* article titled, *"Do Hard Hit Ground Balls Produce More Errors?"*: http://bit.ly/hardgbserrors

The data from the above post analysis suggests errors don't start consistently climbing until Ball Exit Speeds (the speed of the ball coming off the bat) reaches around 95-mph. This data comes from Major League players, by the way.

It goes to show that you have to hit the ball pretty dang hard to force the defense to make an error. To put a 95-mph BES into perspective, **this ball has the ability to travel 380-feet** with an optimal ball launch angle (*1-mph of BES = 4-feet of distance*).

Are your High School hitters hitting even 85 to 90-mph Ball Exit Speeds in games? If not, then maybe you should re-work your ground ball hitting strategy.

The other thing I've heard from Pro-Ground-ball coaches is, *"Well, you can't get a bad hop in the air."* Really!? So you're banking winning versus losing on something out of your control? In other words, you're "hoping" and "praying" for the ground-balls your hitters hit to take a bad hop?! Ridiculous. **Errors are a gift, not something you should expect. And at the higher levels, there are less "gifts".**

Here's a clue, don't focus on things you CANNOT control. Focus on the things you can, which is crushing balls in the air. This is a pitcher's worst nightmare. Where focus goes energy flows.

The "Pro-Ground-ballers", go on and on about...

6

ARGUMENT #6:
COACHES
GORDIE
GILLESPIE AND
AUGIE GARRIDO
STRESS
KEEPING THE
BALL ON THE
GROUND TO
THEIR HITTERS

This is a great example of **making a blanket statement WITHOUT knowing who you're talking to** or not having enough information.

What's interesting to note is after this person said this, and I responded with the following, and they never responded back.

Now, I can't speak for Coach Gordie Gillespie, but here's my connection to Coach Augie Garrido...Coach Garrido played for Fresno State (my alma-mater) back when Coach Pete Beiden (http://www.attheplate.com/wcbl/profile_beiden_pete.html) was the head coach.

I believe, Coach Garrido also played with Coach Bob Bennett (but I could be wrong there), who was my coach the first three years I played at Fresno State. Whether he played with Bennett or not, Coach Garrido learned from Beiden, just as Bennett did. So having never played for Garrido, I have a pretty good idea that **Coach Beiden rubbed off on Garrido** as he did on Bennett.

And Coach Bennett, NEVER told us, in the three years I played for him (and even me – a smaller hitter), to ever hit the ball on the ground...UNLESS I was popping up to much, which is adjustment advice, OR for situational hitting).

So my baseball hitting drills for kids hypothesis with Coach Garrido would echo the same Bennett-Beiden philosophy. I don't think Coach Garrido compiled a collegiate record of 1950-919-9, and has taken his teams to 15 College World Series primarily by instructing his hitters to hit the ball on the ground. Somebody close to Coach Garrido, ask him, and get back to me...PLEASE!

I'm dying to be proven wrong.

Besides, head coaches in the college and professional ranks are generalist. What I mean by that is, they typically don't meddle in hitting or pitching aspects with a fine tooth comb. They have assistant coaches that do those jobs. I can count on one hand how many times, in 3-years, Coach Bennett gave me hitting advice.

Head coaches should be like the CEO of a corporation...**their concern is with big picture strategies**, not on how TPS Reports are suppose to be written.

Well, I commend you for making it this far!

Either you're:

- NOT one of the "Pro-Ground-ballers" anymore, OR
- **You're ONE for a beating!** lol

I assure you this rant is almost over, just a few more holes I need to punch...

The "Pro-Ground-ballers", go on and on about...

7

ARGUMENT #7:
I HAVE TO
TEACH A 5'6",
135-POUND
HIGH SCHOOL
HITTER TO HIT
THE BALL ON
THE GROUND
BECAUSE HIS
BATTED BALL
DISTANCE

MAXES OUT AT 250-FEET!

I'd LOVE to see the look on the face of the High School coach that said this, after I told him on Facebook that **I have two 11yo hitters that hit the ball over 300-feet**, and get this, they did it while weighing less than

Text from dad after 11yo son Orin hit a 300-foot bomb, weighing in at 98-pounds.

100-pounds...AND not just once, but multiple times!!

I'm sure the look was precious.

Obviously, this coach isn't teaching effective mechanics, and doesn't know any better.

I don't care the size of the hitter, I'm going to teach them all how to drive the ball.

Yes, a smaller hitter's role on the team may require them to be better at putting down a sacrifice bunt, hit-and-run, and/or slap hit (especially if they're faster), but ALL hitters will know how to drive the ball.

Driving the ball SHOULD BE the default, NOT hitting the ball on the ground.

And last, but certainly not least...

The "Pro-Ground-ballers", go on and on about...

8

ARGUMENT #8:
EVEN PRO
COACHES AND
"GREAT
HITTING
INSTRUCTORS"
NEVER
PROMOTE
HITTING
FLY-BALLS

This statement is also subjective. Please define "great hitting instructors". Does what Alex Rodriguez and Albert Pujols say about hitting make them a great hitting instructor? Did Ted Williams and Tony Gwynn do a COMPLETE job of analyzing in retrospect, how they did what they did?

Ted Williams came close, but still **was quite far from filling in between the lines** (for me at least). How about Dusty Baker in his hitting book. Mike Schmidt? Charlie Lau?

Look, I'm not putting down any of these legendary people, but we have to have a higher standard than just somebody's hitting "philosophy". We have to teach human movement principles that are validated by science, to hitting a ball. Simple as that.

So, my first baseball hitting drills for kids question to you is, if you believe the above statement, then whose kool-aid are you drinking? Who do you consider a "great hitting instructor"?

And last time I checked on FanGraphs, Ted Williams, Pujols, A-Rod, Mike Trout, Nolan Arenado, Bautista, and Donaldson ARE NOT trying to hit the ball on the ground. Don't believe me? Look at their ground-ball, line drive, fly ball, and home-run to fly-ball ratios. **I guarantee you'll see ALL of them being below average in their ground-balls rates, while being above average in the others.**

Please check...I'll wait.

Oftentimes, what Major League hitters say they're doing is not what we see them do on slow motion analysis. What's *real* and what's *feel* are two totally different things.

I GUARANTEE, most of the effective hitting gurus

online, are telling their hitters to drive the ball IN THE AIR. Again, that includes line drives. NOT on the ground.

Wayne Gretzky image courtesy: http://forum.mmatd.com/

And by the way, **my hitting friends and I may not agree on everything when it comes to hitting, but this we do.**

So you can keep telling yourself these baseball hitting drills for kids stories (i.e. the "Pro-Ground-ballers" statements above), and get mediocre results with your hitters...

Or you can follow what Hockey great Wayne Gretzky says,

*"A good hockey player plays where the puck is. A great hockey player **plays where the puck is going to be.**"*

Teaching hitters to primarily hit ground-balls is 'where the puck is." Teaching them to hit the ball in the air is 'where the puck is going to be'.

If you're not growing, you're dying. Swallow your pride, and come over to the Light Side!

CONCLUSION

Okay, after addressing all the common arguments about teaching hitters to hit ground-balls, you've either accepted the ugly truth about hitting ground-balls, or you NEVER will.

I blame "willful ignorance" for the latter. That's okay. You'll come around eventually, but just remember that I was the one who told you so when you do. lol

For the rest of you, I have a treat...

You may be thinking what I teach my hitters to do since I don't want them hitting ground-balls. I very much agree with the Backspin Tee guys' motto of *'On Path of the Pitch, Bottom Half of the Ball'*. But how do put that into practice?

There are five things I look for in a swing to get the barrel on the plane of the pitch longer, so hitters can hit more consistent line drives:

> 1. Front knee action,
> 2. Back knee action,
> 3. Back foot action,
> 4. Barrel early on plane, and
> 5. Barrel late on plane.

Front Knee Action

There are **six benefits to landing with a bent front leg**:

1. Engaging springy fascia in the legs,
2. Pitch adaptability to off speed pitches,
3. Shrinking the strike zone,
4. Using Ground Reaction Forces,
5. Getting eyes closer to lower pitches in the zone, and
6. **How humans change directions and planes of motion.**

We're not going through all six, but I wanted to highlight the last one...

Please do a YouTube search for: *"armanti edwards route tree session"*, and pay attention to how Armanti Edwards and other NFL wide receivers change direction while doing a "Route Tree Session" with trainer Gari Scott...

Watch them run these routes from a big picture point of view. In other words, not looking for any specific arm or leg angles. **Watch them 'get lower'** when changing directions, or cutting. They land on a bent plant leg, then push off the same leg, extending it, to accelerate again.

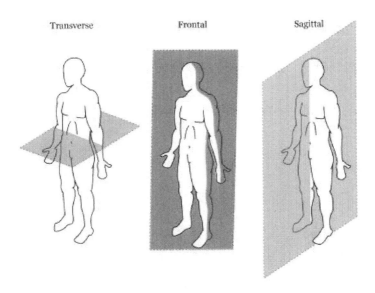

Three main planes of motion. Photo courtesy: goldsgymwebsterny.wordpress.com

There are three main human planes of motion:

1. **Saggital** (front to back motion) – divides the body into right and left halves
2. **Frontal** (a.k.a. side to side motion) – any vertical plane that divides the body into ventral and dorsal (belly and back), and
3. **Transverse** (a.k.a. twisting motion) – is an imaginary plane that divides the body into superior and inferior parts. It is perpendicular to the coronal and sagittal planes.

In changing from one plane of motion to the other, to be effective, there MUST **be a 'getting shorter' of the body's stature**, as the athlete plants and pushes off the ground to change directions.

The wide receivers from the video are changing from the Sagittal (front to back) to Frontal (side to side) Planes. While a hitter changes from the Frontal (side to side) to Transverse (twisting) Planes.

In other words, just like an NFL wide receiver goes from a bent plant leg to straight at push off, a hitter MUST go from a bent landing leg, to a straight leg at 'push off'.

Please CLICK the following link to see the other six benefits: http://gohpl.com/whybentfrontknee

Back Knee Action

Back knee angle during the Final Turn does have a significant impact on ball flight. More bend equals more airtime for the ball. I've seen Little Leaguers to Pro hitters straightening out their back legs during the Final Turn. And they often wonder why they aren't able to drive the ball. Here's why...

Homer Kelly, an aeronautical engineer for Boeing during the Great Depression, said this about knee bend in his book *The Golfing Machine*:

> *"The slant is up in the direction of a straightened Knee.*
> *The slant of the Hips affects the degree of the Hip Turn.*
> *Actually, the primary function of Knee Action – as with*
> *Waist Bend – is to maintain a motionless Head during the*
> *Stroke."*

Homer Kelly's statement has as much to do with hitting as it does with the golf swing! During the Final Turn, a hitter like Adrian Beltre uses his flexed back knee (and straightened front one) to **slant his pelvis up towards the downward traveling pitch,** and as a result, keeps his head motionless during the Final Turn. Early head

movement, pre-stride landing, is okay. Late head movement is not.

Think of the back leg angle as angling your body like a
"ramp".

Please CLICK the following link to see what happened
with a swing experiment where I tested a bent versus
straight back knee during the Final Turn: http://bit.ly/
whybentbackknee

Back Foot Action

I did another swing experiment looking at the difference
in bat speed at impact between 'squishing the bug' with
the back foot and not squishing the bug...basically letting
the back foot skip.

What was the results of the 200 swing experiment?

- **+8-mph difference** in average Impact Bat
  Speed, siding on "Skipping Back Foot",
- +3-mph difference in average Hand Speed Max,
  siding on "Skipping Back Foot",,
- -0.019 difference in average Time To Impact,
  siding on "Skipping Back Foot", and
- **+4-degree difference** in average Attack Angle,
  siding on "Skipping Back Foot"

What does this mean? That 'squishing the bug' is an inferior hitting mechanic. Not ALL elite hitters "skip" the
back foot, but most do "un-weight" it. I just like teaching
my hitters a minimal skip to make sure they're shifting
center mass into impact, behind the front leg. I read
somewhere that Bryce Harper shifts 150% of his body-
weight into impact (skipping his back foot), whereas if he

just "squished the bug", he'd only shift 75% of it. That's a HUGE difference!

Please CLICK the following link to read about the whole swing experiment: http://gohpl.com/whyback-footaction

Barrel Early on Plane

I recently did a video blog post case study featuring one of my 15 year old baseball players Liam titled, *"Taking The Headache Out Of Teaching Barrel Path"*. **We used the Ropebat to change his "Verizon check mark" barrel path into a "Nike Swoosh" sign.**

Why one over the other? I want my hitters to build proper bat lag into their swing, or an early barrel on the plane of the pitch. This helps the hitter barrel the ball more often when their timing may be late.

What's amazing about Liam's transformation was that:

- It only took ten days,
- It took two total 30-minute sessions (beginning of session three was when the AFTER video was taken), and
- **Liam only had access to the Ropebat during our sessions.** After session number-three, his mom went ahead and purchased one for home use.*

Results aren't typical. Liam has a primary "feel" learning style, so the Ropebat worked well for him – and not to mention quickly with minimal use.

Please CLICK the following link to see Liam's full case study transformation: http://gohpl.com/whybarrelearly-onplane

Barrel Late on Plane

The benefit of keeping the barrel on the plane of the pitch longer is to **help the hitter when their timing is early, especially on off-speed and breaking balls.** I typically refer to this as the Power-V, however the V-position of the arms MUST happen AFTER impact. It shouldn't be a goal to get the hitter to Power-V at impact. The latter would put hitters at a disadvantage to inside and higher pitches in the zone.

I also use the coaching cue 'barrel chasing the ball' when teaching this. Please CLICK the following link to a video blog post titled, *"Addison Russell Grand Slam Video: The Anatomy Of A Dinger"*: http://gohpl.com/whybarrel-lateonplane

The last thing I wanted to leave you with besides the Ropebat, as an effective hitting aid to getting the ball in the air, is the Backspin Batting Tee. I mentioned the Backspin Tee swing experiment in one of the earlier rebuttals to the ground-ball argument, but I wanted to share a link to getting the Backspin Tee at my online store (*TheStartingLineupStore.com*): http://gohpl.com/whyback-spintee

I highly recommend these two hitting aids and my *Pitch-Plane Domination* online video course, so you can help hitters to:

- **Increase Batting Average on Balls in Play** (BABIP) – you'll learn how tweaking two simple things can super-charge batted ball distance, which means seeing the backs of outfielders, and not the front!
- **Reduce Strikeouts** (K%) – you'll discover how

to conquer the root cause of striking out and mis-hits, and see coach get excited each time your hitter gets up!

- **Increase Repeatable Power** (OPS) – soak up this one human movement rule and you'll be a pitcher's worst nightmare. The pitcher would be better off, stepping off the mound and throwing the ball in gap!
- **Get More Consistent Multi-Hit Games** – getting 3, 4, and 5-hits in a game is not magic. When all four steps are achieved it makes multi-hit games doable!

Please CLICK the following link to get more information on the *Pitch-Plane Domination* online video course (4-Day Flash Sale where you can **SAVE $30**):

http://gohpl.com/ppdflashsale

If you want to find the Hitting Performance Lab online, then you can at the following places:

- **"Like" us on Facebook** – over 17K+ Likes: https://www.facebook.com/ HittingPerformanceLab/ *(you can also search "Hitting Performance Lab" on Facebook and we'll come up)*
- **Follow us on Twitter** – 3,900+ organic Followers: @hitperformlab (or visit: https://twitter.com/hitperformlab)
- **Subscribe to our YouTube channel** – 3,400+ organic Subscribers: https://www.youtube.com/user/ HittingPerformLab *(you can also search "Hitting Performance Lab" on YouTube and we'll come up)*

- **Connect with Joey on Linkedin** – 500+ connections: https://www.linkedin.com/in/joeymyers30

If you're interested in some of our other online video courses (*over 1,700 SOLD*), then you can learn more at the following link:

http://gohpl.com/hplcourses

If you're interested in the **online lesson training program** *The Feedback Lab*, then you can learn more at the following link:

http://gohpl.com/feedbacklab

For purchasing this book, I want to make you a deal to get access to all my online video courses with the following...

To purchase FOREVER access to all courses and SAVE $91, then please go to the following link:

http://gohpl.com/webinaronlybundle

To take advantage of **low monthly access to ALL courses with a 14-Day $1 Trial**, then please go to the following link:

http://gohpl.com/14daydollartrial

Make sure that you're swinging smarter by moving better ?

And coaches, remember to...

"Go forth and make awesomeness."

– Unknown

HOW TO TEACH 100-POUND HITTERS TO CONSISTENTLY DRIVE THE BALL 300-FEET BOOK

Grab your copy of: *The Catapult Loading System: How To Teach 100-Pound Hitters to Consistently Drive The Ball 300-Feet* book on sale at Amazon today, at the following link:

http://gohpl.com/clsbook

From the back cover:

"My son is 12 and I have used some of the teaching of the Hitting Performance Lab are posting on here and my son hit the ball over 280 feet several times already in the game, not just practices, and also hit the fence on the fly on 300 feet field,

so what this guy is teaching works, a least for my son...He weighs about 110 now but ,what I have noticed is how consistent his power has become thank you so much for your help, **I played 10 years of professional baseball, and I wish I could of used some of this advice."**

– Sandy Arecena

This book is where Bill Nye the Science Guy meets Babe Ruth. Joey Myers uses human movement principles that are validated by science, to hitting a ball. With this system, **Joey and literally hundreds of coaches across the nation are helping baseball and fast pitch hitters, to consistently triple their body-weight in batted ball distance.**

This Step-by-Step guide shows hitting coaches:

- Why hitting philosophy fails and principles that are validated by science succeed
- Why you shouldn't make video analysis FIRST priority when modeling elite hitters
- What 30+ year coaching experience and pro players won't tell you, and how the information source you focus on can dramatically cut down your learning curve
- **How to become a hitting expert when you've never played higher than Little League**
- There's a BIG advantage to learning how the body actually loads (and it's not what you're thinking)
- A simple method that helped Babe Ruth to consistently crush the ball with some of the heaviest bats ever used
- SPECIFIC elite hitters revealing ways to hit high Ball Exit Speeds, swing after swing, using three elements even a 4yo can understand

- At last, the secret to transitioning grooved batting practice swings into game at-bats is revealed

Go to the following link to grab your copy on Amazon:

http://gohpl.com/clsbook

THE SCIENCE
OF STICKY
COACHING:
HOW TO TURN
ORDINARY
ATHLETES INTO
EXTRAORDINARY

Grab your copy of: *The Science Of Sticky Coaching: How To Turn Ordinary Athletes Into Extraordinary* book on sale at Amazon today, at the following link:

http://gohpl.com/soscbook

From the back cover:

Discover How-To Teach, What to Teach, and How Athletes Optimally Learn By Doing What the Top 1% of Coaches Do

This *The Science of Sticky Coaching: How to Turn Ordinary Athletes into Extraordinary* book is split up into three sections:

> 1. **KNOWLEDGE** – (How-To Teach, Doing Things Right, "Effectiveness"): equipping inexperienced coaches, parents, and organizational leaders on how to effectively run their associations and teams,
>
> 2. **LEARNING** – (How they learn) – the science of successful learning, optimizing how young athletes acquire new skills, and maintaining a rich soil for learning, and
>
> 3. **DEVELOPMENT** – (What to teach, Doing the Right Things, "Efficiency"): training crucial fundamentals like playing catch, opposite field hitting, and throwing strikes and locating pitches.

After surveying tens of thousands of my email subscribers, specific thorn-in-the-side frustrations for coaches coaching Little League and 12u softball kept coming up. So this book is an attempt to address all these frustrations using science and what the top 1% of coaches are doing to handle them.

Go to the following link to grab your copy on Amazon: http://gohpl.com/soscbook

ABOUT THE AUTHOR

My Name is Joey Myers, and I'm the founder of the Hitting Performance Lab. I played four years of Division-1 baseball at Fresno State from 2000-2003.

I'm a member of the **American Baseball Coaches Association** (ABCA), the **International Youth and Conditioning Association** (IYCA), and the **Society for American Baseball Research**(SABR). I'm also partnered with the **Positive Coaching Alliance** (PCA).

I'm a certified Youth Fitness Specialist (YFS) through

the International Youth Conditioning Association (IYCA), Corrective Exercise Specialist (CES) through the National Academy of Sports Medicine (NASM), and Vinyasa yoga instructor...AND, I'm also certified in the Functional Muscle Screen (FMS).

I've spent 11+ years in the corrective fitness field, and have a passionate curiosity to help other players – just like yours – dramatically improve performance through the science of human movement.

I'm currently living in Fresno, CA with my wife Tiffany Myers and two kids, Noah (4yo boy) and Gracen (9mo old girl).